SPORTS ZONE

BOYS' LACROSSE

A Guide for Players and Fans

BY MATT CHANDLER

CAPSTONE PRESS

a capstone imprint

Fact Finders Books are published by Capstone
1710 Roe Crest Drive, North Mankato, Minnesota 56003
www.capstonepub.com

Editorial Credits
Lauren Dupuis-Perez, editor; Sara Radka, designer;
Eric Gohl, media researcher; Laura Manthe, production specialist

Photo Credits
Getty Images: 4x6, 18, Batareykin, 12, CDH_Design, cover
(background), CraigRJD, 8, Jamie Sabau, 17, 19, Joe Skipper, 20, Justin
Edmonds, 24, 25, kschulze, 8-9 (background), Omar Rawlings, 22,
Rob Carr, 28, Streeter Lecka, 14, Stringer/Brian A. Westerholt, cover
(foreground), Tetra Images/Erik Isakson, 10-11, Thomas B. Shea,
27, Tom Szczerbowski, 9 (bottom); Newscom: Cal Sport Media/
Eric Canha, 23, Icon SMI/Mike Ridewood, 4; Pixabay: intographics,
background; Shutterstock: David Tran Photo, 29; Wikimedia:
BiblioArchives/LibraryArchives, 9 (top), Gift of Mrs. Joseph Harrison,
Jr./George Catlin, 7 (bottom), Smithsonian American Art Museum, 6

Library of Congress Cataloging-in-Publication Data
Names: Chandler, Matt, author.
Title: Boys' lacrosse: a guide for players and fans / by Matt Chandler.
Description: North Mankato, Minnesota: Capstone Press, 2020. |
Series: Fact finders. Sports zone | Audience: Age 8–9. | Audience: K to
Grade 3.
Identifiers: LCCN 2019005978 | ISBN 9781543574258 (hardcover) |
ISBN 9781543574593 (pbk.) | ISBN 9781543574265 (ebook pdf)
Subjects: LCSH: Lacrosse—Juvenile literature.
Classification: LCC GV989.14 .C53 2020 | DDC 796.36/2—dc23
LC record available at https://lccn.loc.gov/2019005978

All internet sites in the back matter were available and accurate when
this book was sent to press.

Printed and bound in the USA.
PA70

TABLE OF CONTENTS

From 1991 through 2012, the National Lacrosse League's best players, including Gavin Prout and John Tavares, competed in an annual NLL All-Star Game.

Tied 10–10, the 1992 National Lacrosse League (NLL) **championship** went into overtime. The Philadelphia Wings were favored to beat the Buffalo Bandits, who were in their first season. A 23-year-old rookie for the Bandits named John Tavares changed that.

Tavares scooped up a loose ball in front of the Wings' net. He quickly cut to the inside and flipped the ball behind his back, beating the goaltender. The Bandits won the championship. Tavares was a hero!

That was just the beginning for Tavares. He played 23 more seasons for the Bandits. He is the all-time leader in goals scored in NLL history, with 815. Tavares was also the first player in the 32-year history of the 11-team professional lacrosse league to score 500 goals and record 500 assists.

Tavares' love for lacrosse drove him to play year-round. He played in the Canadian Lacrosse Association (CLA) during the NLL offseason. He was part of teams that won six CLA championships!

championship—a contest or tournament that decides which team is the best

LACROSSE HISTORY

The sport of lacrosse has a rich history. Native Americans first played the game as early as the 1400s. Players used a ball and stick to try and score on the opponent's goal. Beyond that, early lacrosse looked much different than it does today.

Modern field lacrosse has 10 players for each team on the field. Native Americans sometimes fielded teams with up to hundreds of men per side! There were also few rules in early lacrosse. Today the sport is all about strategy and speed. Native Americans considered passing and avoiding defenders as cheating. Players carried the ball and challenged defenders to take it away. This led to a very hard-hitting game. Players painted their faces and sticks. They battled violently to win the game.

Lacrosse had spiritual significance to early Native Americans, who believed the game was given to them by the Creator.

Lacrosse got its name from French settlers in America. They used the word *lacrosse* to mean a game played with a curved stick. Before that, each tribe had its own name for the game. The Choctaw called it stick ball. The Mohawk tribes called the game *tewaarathon*, which means "little brother of war." No matter what they called it, the game was an important part of Native American culture more than 600 years ago!

A Game of War

In the 1600s, Native American tribes would sometimes use lacrosse to replace war. Tribes would settle disputes with a game of lacrosse. Although lacrosse was a violent game, it was rare for anyone to die. Tribes lost many men in war. Lacrosse was seen as a better choice.

Today there are two types of lacrosse. Field lacrosse is the traditional game played on a grass field. The field is roughly the size of a football field. Box lacrosse is played indoors, usually in a hockey arena. There are other major differences in the games. Field lacrosse teams have 10 players on the field at once. Box lacrosse has only six players. In lacrosse, the goal is called the **cage**. In field lacrosse it is 6 feet (1.8 meters) wide and 6 feet (1.8 m) tall. A box lacrosse cage is 4 feet (1.2 m) by 4 feet (1.2 m).

cage—the net players try to shoot the ball into in lacrosse

1612

1856

1877

1904

1986

One of the earliest tales of Native American lacrosse is recorded. It describes a match among the Powhatan in Virginia.

The Montreal Lacrosse Club is formed. The club is credited with creating the first written rules for the game.

New York University becomes the first college in the United States to play lacrosse. Today more than 500 colleges field men's and women's lacrosse teams.

Men's lacrosse is played for the first time at the Summer Olympics in St. Louis, Missouri.

USING YOUR HEAD

In the 1600s, Native American lacrosse games began with the ball being bounced off the referee's head. Then the players scrambled to get the ball!

The Eagle Pro Box Lacrosse League is formed in the United States. It later becomes the National Lacrosse League.

GEAR OF THE GAME

When American Robert Roy trotted onto the field in the Netherlands to play in the 1928 Olympic Games, something was different. Roy and his teammates wore leather hats. Their Canadian opponents wore no headgear. This was the first recorded case of lacrosse players wearing helmets for protection. Did it help? Roy's team beat the Canadians, 6–3.

1. Helmet
Helmets are required. They must have a face cage (face mask) and chin strap to protect players.

2. Gloves
Padded gloves protect players' hands from opponents slashing their sticks to knock the ball away.

3. Shoulder/Arm/Rib Pads
Players wear shoulder pads, arm pads, and rib pads under their jerseys. Pads protect against hard hits and ball strikes.

4. Mouthguard
Even though lacrosse helmets have face cages, players are also required to wear a mouthguard.

5. The Crosse
The crosse is a stick with a webbed pocket. It is used for catching, **cradling**, passing, and shooting the ball.

cradling—when a lacrosse player with the ball rocks it back and forth in his stick to control it

Gear for the Game

More teams began wearing leather helmets after the 1928 Olympic Games. By the 1940s, face masks were added. Helmets have changed since then. New technology helps protect players from injury.

Today the helmet is just one piece of the equipment boys' lacrosse players wear on the field. Youth players are also required to wear shoulder pads, a mouthguard, a protective cup, and cleats. Boys' lacrosse allows **checking**. Shoulder pads and a mouthguard are important.

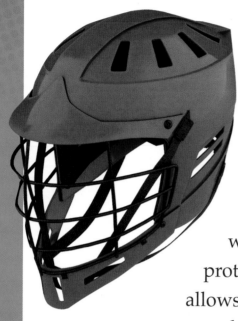

Lacrosse helmet shells are made from strong, lightweight plastic.

Boys' lacrosse sticks are designed with deeper pockets than those used in girls lacrosse. Deeper pockets allow the ball to be thrown much harder. This increases the chance of injury when a player is struck. That's why players wear rib pads, arm pads, and arm guards.

Another important piece of equipment is lacrosse gloves. When a player is carrying the ball up the field, opponents can use their sticks to slap the ball loose. Opponents can also use their sticks to try to knock a player's stick out of his hands. Lacrosse gloves help players grip their sticks. Gloves also protect players' hands against slashing injuries.

Goaltenders add a bit of extra protection. A throat guard is required for all goaltenders. It hangs from the helmet. The throat guard will prevent a hard shot from hitting a goalie in the neck or throat.

The Evolution of the Ball

Lacrosse balls used by some Native American tribes in the 1600s were made of leather. The balls were stuffed with animal hair and sewn shut. Other tribes used balls made of wood. Today balls are made of rubber. Balls come in different sizes depending on the level of play. A standard lacrosse ball measures between 7.75 and 8 inches (19.7 and 20 centimeters). Standard balls weigh about 5 ounces (142 grams).

checking—making contact with another player in order to get the ball away from him or slow him down

LACROSSE RULES

More than 825,000 people in the United States play lacrosse, which is known as the "fastest sport on two feet."

Youth lacrosse is divided into age groups. Each group has unique rules. Twelve- and 13-year-old players play in the 14U group. Games at this level are played on a full-size field. The cages are 6 feet (1.8 m) tall and 6 feet (1.8 m) wide. Each team has 10 players on the field. They are three defensemen, three midfielders, three attackers, and a goaltender.

Games at this level are played in four **quarters**. Each quarter lasts 10 minutes. If a game is tied, the teams play a four-minute overtime. The first team to score in overtime wins the game.

Lacrosse is a fast game. To keep things moving, there are time-related rules. One rule is that a team advancing the ball from its own end only has 20 seconds to cross midfield. This is so the team that is winning can't slow down to use up the clock and win.

quarter—one fourth of a game

Penalties

Players who break the rules can be penalized. They might sit out for one, two, or three minutes. The length of the penalty is decided by the referee. It depends on how bad the action was. Because players can check with their sticks or their bodies, many of the penalties are for rough play. A hit to the neck or head of another player can draw a penalty. Slashing an opponent with your stick or tripping them is also a personal foul. Players who use their stick to check a player can also be penalized. Some stick checking is allowed.

Less serious penalties are called technical fouls. These can include things like entering the **crease** of the opponents' goal or grabbing an opponent and holding him. These penalties can result in 30 seconds off the field. Or possession of the ball might be given to the other team.

crease—the box in front of the lacrosse cage where opposing players are not allowed to be

In men's lacrosse, a player is usually ejected from a game if he has five personal fouls. Players can also be ejected for arguing and fighting.

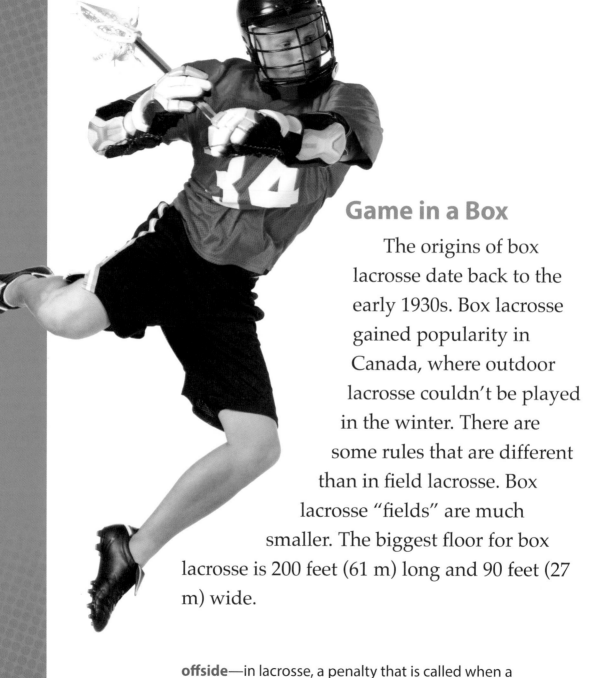

Game in a Box

The origins of box lacrosse date back to the early 1930s. Box lacrosse gained popularity in Canada, where outdoor lacrosse couldn't be played in the winter. There are some rules that are different than in field lacrosse. Box lacrosse "fields" are much smaller. The biggest floor for box lacrosse is 200 feet (61 m) long and 90 feet (27 m) wide.

offside—in lacrosse, a penalty that is called when a defender or attacker crosses the midfield line

During a 2015 major league match, Justin Turri (right) of the Rochester Rattlers checked Kevin Cooper of the Ohio Machine. The Rattlers won the game and tied Ohio for third place in the league.

With four fewer players than field lacrosse, box lacrosse doesn't use defensemen. Instead, there are five players attacking the opponent's goal. There is no rule for **offside**. This leads to a lot more contact in box lacrosse. Players hit opponents much harder than in field lacrosse. There is another unique rule in box lacrosse. Players can "pinch" the ball in their stick. The head of the stick is designed to be narrower. This protects the ball when the player is under attack.

MARATHON GAMES

Youth lacrosse games are typically 40 minutes long. A single Native American game could stretch over two or three days!

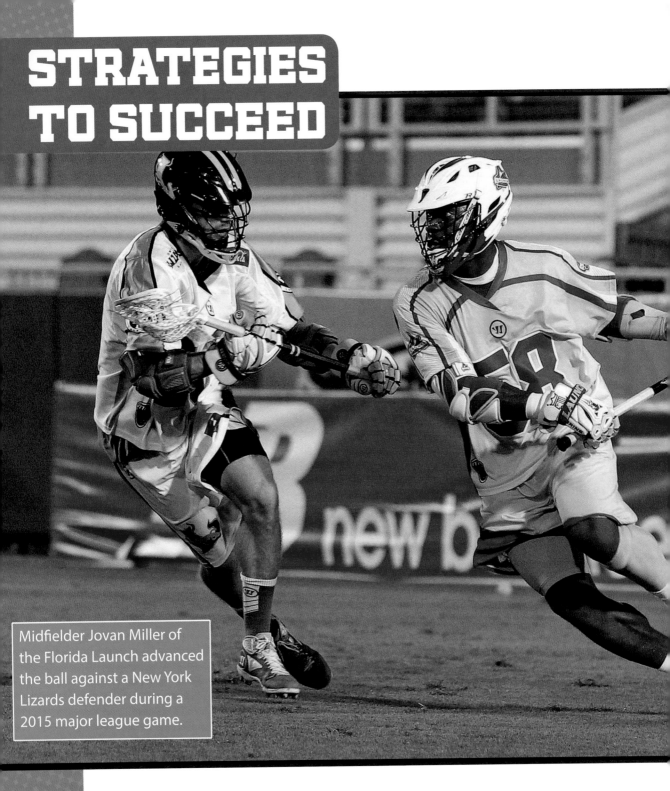

STRATEGIES TO SUCCEED

Midfielder Jovan Miller of the Florida Launch advanced the ball against a New York Lizards defender during a 2015 major league game.

With seconds left in the third quarter of a 2017 game, Denver Outlaws goaltender Jack Kelly intercepted a pass. He fired it downfield. His 80-yard (73-m) shot found the back of the net for a goal!

It's the job of the defensemen to clear the ball when it is trapped in their zone. Although Kelly's goal was awesome, it's rare for a goaltender to score.

Instead, it takes strategy to advance the ball. If a team makes a mistake with the ball in its own end, the opponent is in great position to score. When the goaltender has the ball, his teammates spread out on the field. He may launch the ball downfield hoping for a **breakaway**. He can also dump the ball to a defender nearby. The defender will slowly work it out of the zone. The key strategy is to protect the ball until you cross midfield.

breakaway—in lacrosse, when an offensive player gets past all of the defenders and has a clear shot on goal

Perfect Passing

Passing the ball is a critical part of modern lacrosse. Just like passing a football or basketball, the player has to put the right amount of speed on the ball. A ball flipped too hard can get past the teammate. That might result in a turnover. A soft pass can be intercepted by the defense. The skill of passing is something players spend a lot of time practicing.

Some players prefer bounce passes. Bouncing the ball off the field surface to your teammate can be a very effective way to deliver a pass. Bounce passes can be tough. You have to judge how the ball will bounce off the field surface. The surface might be artificial turf or natural grass. The type of surface can affect the way the ball bounces.

Attacker Ryan Drenner played for the Towson University Tigers before joining Major League Lacrosse (MLL) in 2017.

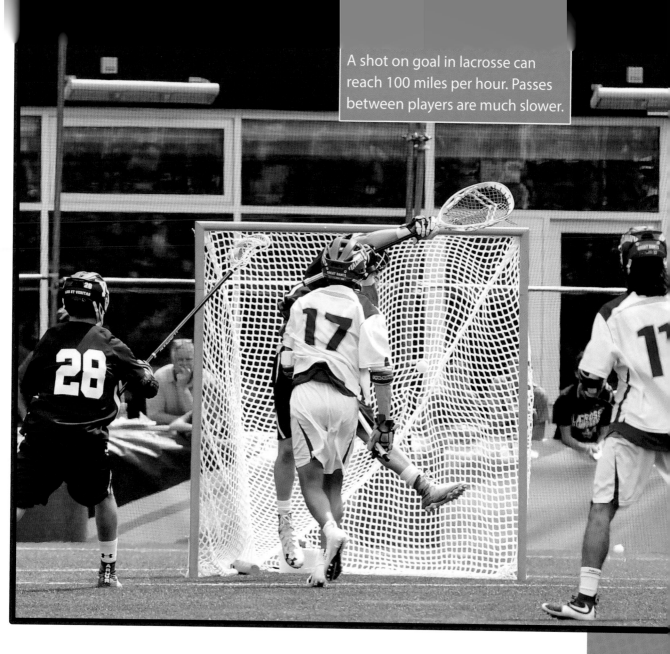

A shot on goal in lacrosse can reach 100 miles per hour. Passes between players are much slower.

Catching and controlling the ball is hard. That's why it is so important to set your teammate up with the perfect pass.

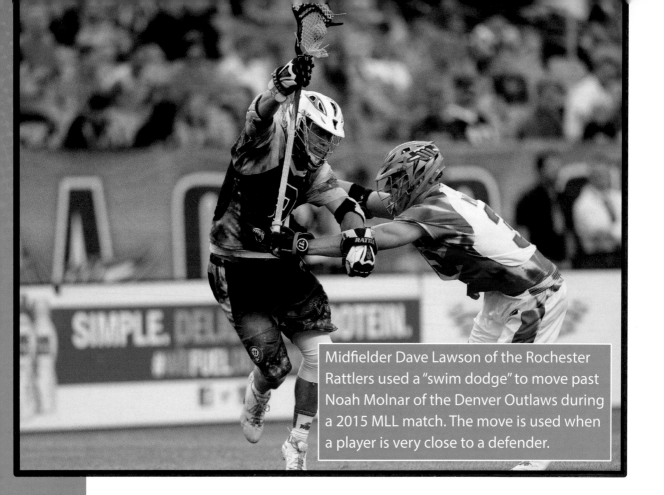

Midfielder Dave Lawson of the Rochester Rattlers used a "swim dodge" to move past Noah Molnar of the Denver Outlaws during a 2015 MLL match. The move is used when a player is very close to a defender.

Strategies for Scoring

It's common for a team to score from 10 to 15 goals in a lacrosse game because they practice strategies to beat the goalie. An attacker can't score if he can't get away from the defender covering him. Players work to **dodge** defenders. Then they can move closer to the goal.

dodge—to avoid something by moving quickly

The real strategy begins once a player has a clear shot on goal. Players that master shot placement are the ones that lead their teams in scoring. There are small spaces to fit your shot in. A strong attacker can see an opening. Then he delivers a lightning-fast shot to the opening before the goalie can cover up. Being around the goal to **rebound** the ball is another way to pick up a goal for your team.

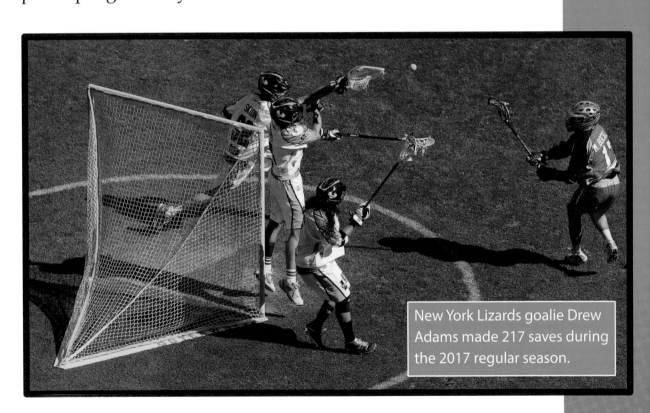

New York Lizards goalie Drew Adams made 217 saves during the 2017 regular season.

rebound—to gain possession of the ball after a missed shot

READY TO PLAY?

The best place to start to learn the game of lacrosse is at your local sporting goods store. An inexpensive stick and a few soft practice balls are all you need to get started. Very young players can even start out using tennis balls to practice catching. Lacrosse players get in the habit of carrying their stick and a ball with them everywhere. There is always a chance to practice cradling the ball, throwing it off a wall, or scooping balls up.

It can also be helpful for young players to watch a lacrosse game to see what it is like. Try and find a high school or college game to attend. See the speed and intensity of the game. This will help you decide if it looks like something you would have fun doing.

Many professional lacrosse games offer a chance for fans to participate in halftime activities.

Joining a Team

Unlike some sports, you don't have to begin playing lacrosse when you are a toddler to be successful. New York Lizards midfielder Paul Rabil didn't pick up a lacrosse stick until he was 12 years old. Today Rabil is an **elite** player. He has won seven championships. The midfielder was named the Most Valuable Player (MVP) in MLL, North America's largest professional field lacrosse league. Rabil set a world record for the fastest lacrosse shot ever recorded. At the 2009 MLL All-Star Game, he ripped a shot 111 miles (179 kilometers) per hour into the net!

Once you are comfortable with ball handling and the basics of the game, find a team. It could be at school or in your community. There is a team out there that is perfect for you!

Lacrosse star Paul Rabil overcame learning challenges as a youth.

LOVING LACROSSE

Boys' lacrosse is one of the fastest-growing team sports in the United States. Today there are more than 450,000 youths playing organized team lacrosse.

elite—describes players who are among the best in the league

Professionals advise the best wall ball workouts last for 20 minutes, with each drill done with both hands—50 times each!

Wall Ball

Catching the ball can be one of the hardest parts of mastering lacrosse. Practicing against a wall can be helpful. Whipping the ball at a wall will improve your reaction as you catch the returning ball. In addition, the ball will come off of the wall at different angles. This helps players judge where the ball is going. Then they can adjust and make the catch.

Glossary

breakaway (*BRAYK-uh-way*)—in lacrosse, when an offensive player gets past all of the defenders and has a clear shot on goal

cage (*KAYJ*)—the net players try to shoot the ball into in lacrosse

championship (*CHAM-pee-uhn-ship*)—a contest or tournament that decides which team is the best

checking (*CHEK-ing*)—making contact with another player in order to get the ball away from him or slow him down

cradling (*KREYD-ling*)—when a lacrosse player with the ball rocks it back and forth in his stick to control it

crease (*KREES*)—the box in front of the lacrosse cage where opposing players are not allowed to be

dodge (*DOJ*)—to avoid something by moving quickly

elite (*i-LEET*)—describes players who are among the best in the league

offside (*OFF-side*)—in lacrosse, a penalty that is called when a defender or attacker crosses the midfield line

quarter (*KWOR-tur*)—one fourth of a game

rebound (*REE-bound*)—to gain possession of the ball after a missed shot

Read More

Editors of Sports Illustrated Kids. *My First Book of Lacrosse.* New York: Sports Illustrated Kids. 2018.

Nagelhout, Ryan. *Lacrosse: Who Does What?* Sports: What's Your Position? New York: Gareth Stevens Publishing, 2018.

Small, Cathleen. *Lacrosse.* Mind vs. Muscle: The Psychology of Sports. New York: Gareth Stevens Publishing, 2019.

Internet Sites

US Lacrosse for youth
www.uslacrosse.org/players/youth

National Lacrosse League
www.nll.com

Lacrosse for beginners
beginnerlacrosse.com

Index